True or False?

Farm Animals

Daniel Nunn

Raintree

Chicago, Illinois

Edited by Dan Nunn, Rebecca Rissman,
and Catherine Veitch
Designed by Joanna Hinton-Malivoire
Picture research by Ruth Blair
Production by Victoria Fitzgerald
Originated by Capstone Global Library
Printed and bound in China by Leo Paper
Products Limited

17 16 15 14 13 12
10 9 8 7 6 5 4 3 2 1

Library of Congress Cataloging-in-Publication Data
Nunn, Daniel.
True or False? Farm animals / Daniel Nunn.
p. cm.—(True or false?)
Includes bibliographical references and index.
ISBN 978-1-4109-5067-3 (hb)—ISBN 978-1-4109-5073-
4 (pb) 1. Domestic animals—Juvenile literature. 2.
Livestock—Juvenile literature. I. Title.
SF75.5.N86 2013
636—dc23   2012019707

Acknowledgments
We would like to thank the following for permission
to reproduce photographs: Shutterstock pp. 4 (© Eric
Isselée), 5 (© Bas Meelker, © grekoff), 6 (© Gail Johnson),
7 (© Eric Isselée), 8 (© gillmar), 9 and back cover
(© Lucie Lang, © Eric Isselée), 10 (© Tsekhmister), 11
(© Valentina_S, © Blinka), 12 (© Popkov), 13 (©
WilleeCole), 14 (© Graeme Knox), 15 (© Igor Sokolov
(breeze)), 16 (© ER_09), 17 (© Winthrop Brookhouse),
18 (© Emese), 19 and back cover (© Subbotina Anna,
© Hitdelight), 20 (© Zotyesz), 21 (© Eric Isselée, © Franck
Boston), 22 (© Blue Ice).

Cover photographs reproduced with permission of
Shutterstock (© Valentina_S (chicken), © Blinka (milk),
© Patryk Kosmider (nest)).

Every effort has been made to contact copyright holders
of any material reproduced in this book. Any omissions
will be rectified in subsequent printings if notice is given
to the publisher.

Contents

Farm Animals 4

Sheep 5

Cats. 7

Cows 9

Chickens 11

Dogs 13

Pigs 15

Horses 17

Bees 19

Llamas 21

Can You Remember?. 23

Index, Activity 24

Farm Animals

A farm animal is an animal that lives or works on a farm. How much do **YOU** know about farm animals?

Sheep

Wool comes from a sheep.

✔ **True** or false? ✗

5

✓ True!

Wool comes from a sheep. Farmers shear the sheep to get the wool.

Cats

Cats help
farmers
knit wool.

 True or false?

✖ **False!**

Farmers keep cats to catch mice and rats. The cats help keep farms clean.

8

Cows

Cows lay eggs.

 True or **false?**

✖ False!

Cows do not lay eggs. Hens, ducks, geese, and other birds lay eggs.

Chickens

Milk comes from
a chicken.

 True or false?

✕ False!

Chickens do not make milk. Most of the milk we drink comes from cows.

Dogs

Some dogs work on farms.

True or **false?**

13

✓ **True!**

Some dogs work as sheepdogs. They help farmers move sheep around.

Pigs

Baby pigs are called "puppies."

✔ True **or** false? ✗

✖ False!

Baby pigs are called piglets. Pigs and piglets roll in the mud to keep cool!

Horses

Some horses work on farms.

 True or false?

✔ True!

Some horses pull plows or carts on farms. But today, most farms use tractors!

Bees

Bees on a farm make wool
for sweaters.

 True or false?

✖ False!

Some farmers DO keep bees. But the bees make honey, not wool! The bees live in homes called hives.

Llamas

Some farmers keep llamas to make them pajamas.

True or **false?** ✓ ✗

✖ False!

But llamas do have woolly coats.
Farmers shear them like sheep.

Can You Remember?

Which animal lays eggs?

Which animal makes milk?

Which animal makes honey?

Look back through the book to check your answers.

Index

baby pigs 15, 16

eggs 9, 10, 23

honey 20, 23

milk 11, 12, 23

plows 18

sheepdogs 14

tractors 18

wool 5, 6, 7, 19, 20, 22

Activity

Make Your Own True or False Game

Help your child make a Farm Animals: True or False game. Collect a selection of pictures of farm animals from magazines. Mount each picture on cardboard. Then with the child, write a series of true or false statements about the farm animals in the pictures, on separate pieces of cardboard. Put one statement with each corresponding picture. On the back of each picture, write if the statement is true or false. For the game, read the statement out loud, ask the child if it is true or false, then have the child turn over the picture to check if he or she is correct. To extend the activity, ask the child to write the statements and whether they are true or false, and then ask you the questions.